NOBEL
LECTURE

Isaac Bashevis Singer

NOBEL
LECTURE

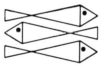

Farrar Straus Giroux

NEW YORK

Copyright © 1978 by The Nobel Foundation
Yiddish text copyright © 1978 by Isaac Bashevis Singer
Special contents of this edition copyright © 1979
by Farrar, Straus and Giroux, Inc.
First printing, 1979
Printed in the United States of America
Published simultaneously in Canada by
McGraw-Hill Ryerson Ltd., Toronto
Designed by Guy Fleming
Library of Congress Cataloging in Publication Data
Singer, Isaac Bashevis.
Nobel lecture.
Text of the lecture is in English and
Yiddish.
1. Singer, Isaac Bashevis.
—Criticism and interpretation—Addresses,
essays, lectures.   I. Title.
PJ5129.S49Z93   839'.09'33   79–11568

Contents

NOBEL
LECTURE

THE STORYTELLER and poet of our time, as in any other time, must be an entertainer of the spirit in the full sense of the word, not just a preacher of social or political ideals. There is no paradise for bored readers and no excuse for tedious literature that does not intrigue the reader, uplift his spirit, give him the joy and the escape that true art always grants. Nevertheless, it is also true that the serious writer of our time must be deeply concerned about the problems of his generation. He cannot but see that the power of religion, especially belief in revelation, is weaker today than it was in

3]

any other epoch in human history. More and more children grow up without faith in God, without belief in reward and punishment, in the immortality of the soul, and even in the validity of ethics. The genuine writer cannot ignore the fact that the family is losing its spiritual foundation. All the dismal prophecies of Oswald Spengler have become realities since the Second World War. No technological achievements can mitigate the disappointment of modern man, his loneliness, his feeling of inferiority, and his fear of war, revolution and terror. Not only has our generation lost faith in Providence, but also in man himself, in his institutions, and often in those who are nearest to him.

In their despair a number of those who no longer have confidence in the leadership of our society look up to the writer, the master of words. They hope against hope that the man of talent and sensitivity can perhaps rescue civilization. Maybe there is a spark of the prophet in the artist after all.

As the son of a people who received the worst blows that human madness can inflict, I have many times resigned myself to never finding a true way out. But a new hope always emerges, telling me that it is not yet too late for all of us to take stock and make a decision. I was brought up to believe in free will. Although I came to doubt all revelation, I can never accept the idea that the universe is a physical or chemical accident, a result of blind evolution. Even though I learned to recognize the lies, the clichés, and the idolatries of the human mind, I still cling to some truths which I think all of us might accept someday. There must be a way for man to attain all possible pleasures, all the powers and knowledge that nature can grant him, and still serve God—a God who speaks in deeds, not in words, and whose vocabulary is the universe.

I am not ashamed to admit that I belong to those who fantasize that literature is capable of bringing new horizons and new perspectives—philosophical, religious, aesthetical, and even social. In the history of old Jewish literature there was never any basic difference between the poet and the prophet. Our ancient poetry often became law and a way of life.

Some of my cronies in the cafeteria near the *Jewish Daily Forward* in New York call me a pessimist and a decadent, but there is always a background of faith behind resignation. I found comfort in such pessimists and decadents as Baudelaire, Verlaine, Edgar Allan Poe, and Strindberg. My interest in psychic research made me find solace in such mystics as your Swedenborg and in our own Rabbi Nachman Bratzlaver, as well as in a great poet of my time, my friend Aaron Zeitlin, who died a few years ago and left a spiritual inheritance of high quality, most of it in Yiddish.

The pessimism of the creative person is not decadence, but a mighty passion for the redemption of man. While the poet entertains he continues to search for eternal truths, for the essence of being. In his own fashion he tries to solve the riddle of time and change, to find an answer to suffering, to reveal love in the very abyss of cruelty and injustice. Strange as these words may sound, I often play with the idea that when all the social theories collapse and wars and revolutions leave humanity in utter gloom, the poet—whom Plato banned from his Republic—may rise up to save us all.

[*Mr. Singer read the following paragraph in Yiddish, at the start of the lecture.*]

The high honor bestowed upon me by the Swedish Academy is also a recognition of the Yiddish language—a language of exile, without a land, without frontiers, not supported by any government, a language which possesses no words for weapons, ammunition, military exercises, war tactics; a language that was despised by both gentiles and emancipated Jews. The truth is that what the great religions preached, the Yiddish-speaking people of the ghettos practiced day in and day out. They were the people of the Book in the truest sense of the word. They knew of no greater joy than the study of man and human relations, which they called Torah, Talmud, Musar, Kabbalah. The ghetto was not only a place of refuge for a persecuted minority but a great experiment in peace, in self-discipline, and in humanism. As such, a residue still exists and refuses to give up in spite of all the brutality that surrounds it.

I was brought up among those people. My father's home on Krochmalna Street in Warsaw was a study house, a court of justice, a house of prayer, of storytelling, as well as a place for weddings and Hasidic banquets. As a child I had heard from my older brother and master, I. J. Singer, who later wrote *The Brothers Ashkenazi*, all the arguments that the rationalists from Spinoza to Max Nordau brought out against religion. I have heard from my father and my mother all the answers that faith in God could offer to those who doubt and search for the truth. In our home and in many other homes the eternal questions were more actual than the latest news in the Yiddish newspaper. In spite of all the disenchantments and all my skepticism, I believe that the nations can learn much from those Jews, their way of thinking, their way of bringing up children, their finding happiness where others see nothing but misery and humiliation.

To me the Yiddish language and the conduct of those who spoke it are identical. One can find in the Yiddish tongue and in the Yiddish style expressions of pious joy, lust for life, longing for the Messiah, patience, and deep appreciation of human individuality. There is a quiet humor in Yiddish and a gratitude for every day of life, every crumb of success, each encounter of love. The Yiddish mentality is not haughty. It does not take victory for granted. It does not demand and command but it muddles through, sneaks by, smuggles itself amid the powers of destruction, knowing somewhere that God's plan for Creation is still at the very beginning.

8]

There are some who call Yiddish a dead language, but so was Hebrew called for two thousand years. It has been revived in our time in a most remarkable, almost miraculous way. Aramaic was certainly a dead language for centuries, but then it brought to light the Zohar, a work of mysticism of sublime value. It is a fact that the classics of Yiddish literature are also the classics of the modern Hebrew literature. Yiddish has not yet said its last word. It contains treasures that have not been revealed to the eyes of the world. It was the tongue of martyrs and saints, of dreamers and Kabbalists—rich in humor and in memories that mankind may never forget. In a figurative way, Yiddish is the wise and humble language of us all, the idiom of frightened and hopeful humanity.

Nobel Prize Citation

"The Nobel Prize for Literature to
Isaac Bashevis Singer
for his impassioned narrative art which,
with roots in a Polish-Jewish cultural tradition,
brings universal human conditions to life."

Why I Write for Children

[This statement, originally prepared by Mr. Singer for the occasion of his acceptance of the National Book Award in 1970 for *A Day of Pleasure: Stories of a Boy Growing Up in Warsaw*, was read to the assembled guests at the Nobel Prize banquet at the City Hall in Stockholm on December 10, 1978]

THERE ARE FIVE HUNDRED REASONS why I began to write for children, but to save time I will mention only ten of them.

Number 1. Children read books, not reviews. They don't give a hoot about the critics.

Number 2. Children don't read to find their identity.

Number 3. They don't read to free themselves of guilt, to quench their thirst for rebellion, or to get rid of alienation.

Number 4. They have no use for psychology.

Number 5. They detest sociology.

Number 6. They don't try to understand Kafka or *Finnegans Wake*.

Number 7. They still believe in God, the family, angels, devils, witches, goblins, logic, clarity, punctuation, and other such obsolete stuff.

Number 8. They love interesting stories, not commentary, guides, or footnotes.

Number 9. When a book is boring, they yawn openly, without any shame or fear of authority.

Number 10. They don't expect their beloved writer to redeem humanity. Young as they are, they know that it is not in his power. Only the adults have such childish illusions.

The Work of

ISAAC BASHEVIS SINGER

BY PROFESSOR LARS GYLLENSTEN

Permanent Secretary of the Swedish Academy

"HEAVEN AND EARTH conspire that everything which has been, be rooted out and reduced to dust. Only the dreamers, who dream while awake, call back the shadows of the past and braid from unspun threads unspun nets." These words from one of Isaac Bashevis Singer's stories in the collection *The Spinoza of Market Street* (1961) say quite a lot about the writer himself and this narrative art.

Singer was born in a small town or village in eastern Poland and grew up in one of the poor, overpopulated Jewish quarters of Warsaw, before and during the First World War. His father was a rabbi of the Hasid school of piety, a spiritual mentor for a motley collection of people who sought his help. Their language was Yiddish—the language of the simple people and of the mothers, with its sources far back in the Middle Ages and with an influx from several different cultures with which this people had come in contact during the many centuries they had been scattered abroad. It is Singer's language. And it is a storehouse which has gathered fairy tales and anecdotes, wisdom, superstitions, and memories for hundreds of years past, through a history that seems to have left nothing untried in the way of adventures and afflictions. The Hasid piety was a kind of popular Jewish mysticism. It could merge into prudery and petty-minded, strict adherence to the law. But it could also open out towards orgiastic frenzy and messianic raptures or illusions.

This world was that of East European Jewry—at once very rich and very poor, peculiar and exotic but also familiar with all human experience behind its strange garb. This world has now been laid waste by the most violent of all the disasters that have overtaken the Jews and other people in Poland. It has been rooted out and reduced to dust. But it comes alive in Singer's writings, in his waking dreams, his very waking dreams, clear-sighted and free of illusion but also full of broad-mindedness and unsentimental compassion. Fantasy and experience change shape. The evocative power of Singer's inspiration acquires the stamp of reality, and reality is lifted up by dreams and imagination into the sphere of the supernatural, where nothing is impossible and nothing is sure.

Singer began his writing career in Warsaw in the years between the wars. Contact with the secularized environment and the surging social and cultural currents involved a liberation from the setting in which he had grown up—but also a conflict. The clash between tradition and renewal, between otherworldliness and pious mysticism on the one hand, free thought, doubt, and nihilism on the other, is an essential theme in Singer's short stories and novels. Among many other themes, it is dealt with in Singer's family chronicles—the novels *The Family Moskat*, *The Manor*, and *The Estate*, from the 1950s and 1960s. These extensive epic works depict how old Jewish families are broken up by the new age and its demands and how they are split, socially and humanly. The author's apparently inexhaustible psychological fantasy and insight have created a microcosm, or rather a well-populated micro-chaos, out of independent and graphically convincing figures.

Singer's earliest fictional works, however, were not big novels but short stories and novellas. The novel *Satan in Goray* appeared in 1935, when the Nazi terror was threatening and just before the author emigrated to the United States, where he has lived and worked ever since. It treats of a theme to which Singer has often returned in different ways—the false Messiah, his seductive arts and successes, the mass hysteria around him, his fall and the breaking up of illusions in destitution and new illusions or in penance and purity. *Satan in Goray* takes place in the seventeenth century after the cruel ravages of the Cossacks with outrages and mass murder of Jews and others. The book anticipates what was to come in *our* time. These people are not wholly evil, not wholly good—they are haunted and harassed by things over which they have no control, by the force of circumstances and by their own passions—something alien but also very close.

This is typical of Singer's view of humanity—the power and fickle inventiveness of obsession, the destructive but also inflaming and creative potential of the emotions, and their grotesque wealth of variation. The passions can be of the most varied kinds —often sexual, but also fanatical hopes and dreams, the figments of terror, the lure of lust or power, the nightmares of anguish. Even boredom can become a restless passion, as with the main character in the tragicomic picaresque novel *The Magician of Lublin* (1961), a kind of Jewish Don Juan and rogue, who ends up as an ascetic or saint. In a sense, a counterpart to this book is *The Slave* (1962), really a legend of a lifelong, faithful love which becomes a compulsion, forced into fraud despite its purity, heavy to bear though sweet, saintly but with the seeds of shamefulness and deceit. The saint and the rogue are near of kin.

Singer has perhaps given of his best as a consummate storyteller and stylist in the short stories and in the numerous and fantastic novellas, available in English translation in about a dozen collections. The passions and crazes are personified in these strange tales as demons, specters, and ghosts, all kinds of infernal or supernatural powers from the rich storehouse of Jewish popular belief or of his own imagination. These demons are not only graphic literary symbols but also real, tangible forces. The Middle Ages seem to spring to life again in Singer's works, the daily round is interwoven with wonders, reality is spun from dreams, the blood of the past pulsates in the present. This is where Singer's narrative art celebrates its greatest triumphs and bestows a reading experience of a deeply original kind, harrowing but also stimulating and edifying. Many of his characters step with unquestioned authority into the pantheon of literature where the eternal companions and mythical figures live, tragic and grotesque, comic and touching, weird and wonderful—people of dream and torment, baseness and grandeur.

די נאָבעל רעדע

נסים. אראמעאיש איז זיכער געוואָרן באַטראכט ווי טויט.
אָבער אין דעם דאָזיקן טויטן לשון איז געוואָרן געשריבן
דער זוהר, אַ מיסטיש ווערק פון הימלישער פראכט.
ס׳איז אַ פאקט אז די קלאסיקער פון אידיש זענען אויך
די קלאסיקער פון מאָדערנעם העברעאיש. אידיש האָט
נאָך ווייט נישט געזאָגט דאָס לעצטע וואָרט. עם אַנט-
האלט אוצרות וואָס זענען נאָך נישט אנטדעקט פאר
דער גרויסער וועלט. עס איז אַ לשון פון מאַרטירער
און קדושים, פון טרוימער און מקובלים — רייך אין
הומאָר און אין זכרונות, וואָס דער מין מענטש טאָר
נישט פארגעסן. אין אַ פיגוראטיוון זין איז אידיש דאָס
קלוגע און אונטערטעניקע לשון פון אונז אַלעמען,
דער אידיאָם פון דער דערשראָקענער און האָפנדיקער
מענטשהייט.

23]

געקוקט אויף אַלע מײַנע אַנטוישונגען און מײַן גאַנצן
סקעפּטיציזם, גלויב איך אַז די פֿעלקער קענען אַ סך
לערנען פֿון די דאָזיקע אידן; זייער געדאַנקען־גאַנג,
זייער אופֿן פֿון דערציען קינדער, זייער געפֿינען גליק
דאָרעם װאו אַנדערע זעען בלויז אומגליק און דערנידערונג.

פֿאַר מיר איז אידיש ענג פֿאַרבונדן מיט יענע
װאָס האָבן גערעדט דאָס דאָזיקע לשון. מ'קאַן געפֿינען
אין גײַסט פֿון אידיש װאַרע פֿרייד, לוסט צום לעבן, די
בענקשאַפֿט נאָך משיח, געדולד צו װאַרטן און אַ טיפֿע
אָפּשאַצונג פֿון מענטשלעכער אינדיװידואַליטעט. ס'איז
פֿאַראַן אַ שטילער הומאָר אין אידיש, אַ דאַנקבאַרקייט
פֿאַר יעדן טאָג װאָס מען בלייבט לעבן, פֿאַר יעדן ברעקל
הצלחה, פֿאַר יעדער באַגעגעניש מיט ליבשאַפֿט. אידיש
איז נישט גאװה'דיק, נישט זיכער מיט נצחון. אידיש
פֿאָדערט נישט און קעמפֿט נישט, נאָר קומט־איבער,
לעבט־אַדורך, שמוגלט זיך אַדורך צווישן די כּוחות פֿון
צעשטערונג, וויסנדיק דערבײַ אַז גאָט'ס פּלאַן פֿאַר דער
באַשאַפֿונג איז ערשט אין סאַמע אָנהויב.

ס'זענען פֿאַראַן אַזוינע װאָס רופֿן אָן אידיש אַ
טויטע שפּראַך. אָבער מ'האָט אויך געהאַלטן קנאַפּע
צװיי טויזנט יאָר צײַט העברעאיש פֿאַר אַ טויטער
שפּראַך. מיט אַמאָל איז העברעאיש אויפֿגעשטאַנען
תחית־המתים אויף אַ װאונדערלעכן אופֿן, ממש דורך

די נאָבעל רעדע

לערנען זוגען מענטשן און מענטשעלעכע באַציאונגען
וואָס זיי האָבן אָנגערופן תורה, תלמוד, מוסר, קבלה.
די געטאָ איז געווען נישט בלויז אן אָרט פון אַנטרינונג
פאַר אַ פאַרפאָלגטער מינאָריטעט, נאָר אויך אַ גרויסער
עקספּערימענט אין שלום, זעלבסט־דיסציפּלין און הו־
מאַניזם. רעשטלעכער דערפון עקזיסטירן ביז היינט צו
טאָג, נישט געקוקט אויף דער גאַנצער ברוטאַליטעט
וואָס רינגלט זיי אַרום.

איך בין דערצויגן געוואָרן צווישן אַזוינע אידן.
מיין פאַטער'ס הויז איז אויף קראָכמאַלנע גאַס אין וואַרשע
איז געווען סײ אַ בית־מדרש, סײ אַ בית־דין־שטוב, אן
אָרט וואו מען האָט דערציילט מעשה'ס און וואו מ'האָט
געפראַוועט חתונה'ה'ס און חסידישע סעודה'לעך. ווען איך
בין געווען אַ קינד האָב איך געהערט פון מיין ברודער
און מייסטער י. י. זינגער — וואָס האָט שפּעטער אַנגע־
שריבן ,,די ברידער אַשכנזי'' — אַלע אַרגומענטן וואָס
די ראַציאָנאַליסטן, פון שפּינאָזאַ ביז מאַקס נאָרדוי, האָבן
אַרויסגעטראָגן קעגן רעליגיע. פון מיין פאַטער און
מוטער האָב איך געהערט אַלע ענטפערס וואָס דער
גלויבן אין גאָט קאָן געבן יענע וואָס צווייפלען און
זוכן דעם אמת. אין אונזער היים און אין אַ סך אַנדערע
היימען זענען די אייביקע פראַגן געווען מער אַקטועל
ווי די לעצטע נייעס פון דער אידישער צייטונג. נישט

25]

אַזוי זוכט ער אייביקע אמת׳ן, דעם עסענץ פון דאַזיין.
ער פרואװט אויף זיין אייגענעם שטייגער צו באַשיידן
דאָס רעטעניש פון צייט און פאַרענדערונג, געפינען אַן
ענטפער אויף ליידן, אַנטפלעקן ליבע אין סאַמע תהום
פון אכזריות און אומגערעכטיקייט. װי אויסטערליש די
װערטער זאָלן אייך נישט קלינגען, איך שפיל מיך אָסט
מיט דעם געדאַנק, אַז װען אַלע סאָציאַלע טעאָריעס
װעלן זיך פונאַנדערפאַלן און מלחמות און רעװאָלוציעס
װעלן איבערלאָזן די מענטשהייט אין פולשטענדיקער
פאַרצװייפלונג, װעט דער פּאָעט — יענער װאָס פּלאַטאָ
האָט אים פאַרטריבן פון זיין רעפּובליק — אויפשטיין
און ראַטעװען אונז אַלע.

דער גרויסער כבוד װאָס די שװעדישע אַקאַ־
דעמיע האָט מיר אָנגעטאָן איז אויך אַן אָנערקענונג
פון אידיש — אַ שפּראַך פון גלות, אָן אַ לאַנד, אָן
גרענעצן, נישט אונטערגעשטיצט פון קיין שום רע־
גירונג; אַ שפּראַך װאָס פאַרמאָגט כמעט נישט קיין
װערטער פאַר װאָפֿן, אמוניציע, מיליטערישע איבונגען
און טאַקטיק; אַ לשון װאָס איז געװאָרן פאַראַכטעט
סאַי פון גויים און סאַי פון רוב עמאַנציפּירטע אידי.
דער אמת איז, אַז װאָס די גרויסע רעליגיעס האָבן
געפּרעדיקט האָבן די אידן אין געטאָ פּראַקטיצירט.
זיי האָבן נישט געהאַט קיין גרעסערע פרייד װי

ברענגען נייע האָריזאָנטן און נייע פּערספּעקטיוון —
פילאָזאָפישע, רעליגיעזע, עסטעטישע און אַפילו סאָציאַלע.
אין דער געשיכטע פון דער אַלטער אידישער ליטעראַ־
טור איז קיינמאָל נישטאָ קיין גרינטלעכער אונטערשייד
צווישן פּאָעזיע און נבואה. אונזער פּאָרצייטיקע פּאָעזיע
איז געוואָרן פאַרוואַנדלט אין דינים און אין אַ לעבנס־
שטייגער.

אייניקע פון מיינע קאָלעגן אין דער קאָפּעטעריע
נעבן דעם „פאָרווערטס" האָבן מיך אָנגערופן אַ פּעסי־
מיסט און אַ דעקאַדענט, אָבער פאַקטיש איז אַלעמאָל
פאַראַן אַ הינטערגרונד פון אמונה הינטער רעזיגנאַציע.
איך האָב געפונען טרייסט אין אַזוינע פּעסימיסטן און
דעקאַדענטן ווי באָדלער, ווערלען, עדגאַר אַלאַן פּאָ און
סטרינדבערג. מיין אינטערעס אין פּסיכישער פאָרשונג
האָט געוויזקט אַז איך האָב געפונען אַ נחמה אין אַזוינע
מיסטיקער ווי סוועדענבאָרג און ר' נחמן בראַצלאָווער,
ווי אויך אין אַ גרויסן פּאָעט פון מיין צייט, מיין פריינד
אהרן צייטלין, וואָס איז געשטאָרבן מיט אַ פּאָר יאָר
צוריק און איבערגעלאָזט נאָך זיך אַ גייסטיקע ירושה
פון הויכן קוואַליטעט, ס'רוב אין אידיש.

דער פּעסימיזם פון דעם שעפּערישן מענטש איז
נישט דעקאַדענץ, נאָר אַ מעכטיקער פאַרלאַנג פאַר
גאולה פון מין מענטש. אַזוי ווי דער פּאָעט פאַרווייַלט,

ערגסטע קלעפּ וואָס די מענטשלעכע אכזריות און משוגעת
קאָנען דערלאַנגען, מוז איך טראַכטן וועגן די סכנה'ס
וואָס לויערן אויף אונזער וועלט. איך האָב מיך וויפל
מאָל מייאש געוואָרן אין יעדער הילף. אָבער יעדעם מאָל
האָט זיך אויפגעוועקט אין מיר די האָפענונג, אַז אפשר
איז נאָך נישט צו-שפּעט פֿאַר אונז אַלעמען זיך אַפּצוגעבן
אַ חשבון-הנפש און צו קומען צו אַ שלום. איך בין
דערצויגן געוואָרן אין דער אמונה אין פֿרייען ווילן. איך
צווייפל אין אַנטפּלעקונגען, אָבער איך קאָן קיינמאָל
נישט אָננעמען אַז דער אוניווערז איז אַ פֿיזישער אָדער
כעמישער צופֿאַל, אַ רעזולטאַט פֿון בלינדער עוואָלוציע.
איך זע אויף מיין אייגענעם שטייגער די ליגנם, די
שאַבלאָנען און די אָפּגעטערי פֿון מענטשלעכן געדאַנק,
אָבער איך קלאַמער מיך נאָך אַלץ אין אַ צאָל אמת'ן
וואָס דאָס מענטשלעכע מין קאָן זיי אָננעמען און אויף
זיי בויען. ס'איז פֿאַראַן, זאָג איך מיר, אַ וועג ווי אַזוי
דער מענטש זאָל קאָנען געניסן אַלע מעגלעכע פֿאַרגע-
ניגנם, אַלע כּוחות און יעדעם וויסן וואָס די נאַטור
שענקט אונז און דערבײ דינען גאָט — אַ גאָט וואָס
רעדט מיט מעשׂים, נישט מיט ווערטער און וואָס זיין
ווערטערבוך איז דער קאָסמאָס.

איך שעם מיך נישט מודה צו זיין אַז איך געהער
צו יענע וואָס פֿאַנטאַזירן, אַז די ליטעראַטור קאָן אונז

געטלעכער אָנטפּלעקונג, איז שוואַכער היינט ווי אין
וועלכער ס'איז עפּעס פון דער געשיכטע. גרויסע צאָלן
קינדער ווערן דערצויגן אָן אמונה אין גאָט, לוין און
שטראָף, דער אוממשטערבלעכקייט פון דער נשמה און
אַפילו אין די פּרינציפּן פון עטיק. דער שרייבער קאָן
נישט פאַרזען דעם פאַקט אז די פאַמיליע פאַרלירט אַלץ
מער און מער איר גייסטיקן פונדאַמענט. אַלע שוואַרצע
נבואות פון אַסוואָלד שפּענגלער ווערן מקויים זינט דעם
צווייטן וועלט־קריג. קיין שום טעכנאָלאָגישע דערגריי־
כונגען קאָנען נישט מילדערן די טיפע אַנטוישונג פון
דעם היינטיקן מענטש, זיין געפיל פון איינזאַמקייט,
מינדערווערטיקייט, זיין פחד פאַר מלחמה, רעוואָלוציע,
טעראָר. נישט בלויז האָט אונזער דור פאַרלוירן דעם
גלויבן אין השגחה, נאָר אויך אין זיך אַליין, זיינע
אינסטיטוציעס און אַפילו אויך אין זיינע נאָענטסטע.

אַ צאָל פון יענע וואָס האָבן אָנגעוואוירן דעם
צוטרוי צו דער סאָציאַלער און פּאָליטישער פירערשאַפט
פון אונזער געזעלשאַפט פרואוון אין זייער פאַרצווייפלונג
זוכן אַן אָנלען אין דעם שרייבער, אין דעם מייסטער פון
ווערטער, אפשר ווער ער, דער מענטש פון טאַלאַנט
און סענסיוויטעט, ראָטעווען די ציוויליזאַציע; אפשר
איז פאַרט פאַראַן אין דעם קינסטלער אַ פונק פון נבואה.

ווי אַ זון פון אַ פאָלק, וואָס האָט געקראָגן די

אידיש לעבן–אַ מוסטער
פֿאַר אַלע פֿעלקער

נאָבעל לעקציע געהאַלטן אין דער שוועדישער
אַקאַדעמיע דעם 8טן דעצעמבער, 1978, אין
שטאָקהאָלם. — מיט דעם איינגעצויגענעם
פֿאַראַגראַף האָט יצחק באַשעוויס אָנגעהויבן
די לעקציע אויף אידיש.

דער דערציילער פֿון אונזער צייט, ווי פֿון אַלע
צייטן, מוז זיין און פֿאַרבלייבן אַ פֿאַרווײַלער אין בעסטן
זין פֿון וואָרט, נישט אַ פֿאַרשפּרייטער פֿון פּאָליטישע
אָדער סאָציאַלע אידעאַלן. ס'איז נישטאָ קיין גן־עדן פֿאַר
פֿאַרלאַנגגוויילוקטע לייענער און קיין שום פֿאַרענטפֿערונג
פֿאַר ליטעראַטור וואָס אינטערעסירט נישט דעם לייענער,
דערהויבט נישט זיין געמיט, גיט אים נישט די פֿרייד
און די פֿאַרגעסונג וואָס וואָרע קונסט גיט אונז. ס'איז
פֿונדעסטוועגן אויך אמת אַז דער ערנסטער שרייבער
פֿון אונזער צייט מוז זיין טיף אינטערעסירט אין די
פּראָבלעמען פֿון זיין דור. ער מוז איינזען, צום ביישפּיל,
אַז דער כּח פֿון רעליגיע, ספּעציעל דער גלויבן אין

יצחק באַשעוויס זינגער

די נאַבעל רעדע

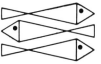

פאראר שטראוס זשירו

ניו יאָרק

די נאָבעל
רעדע

———————————————